D0746806

A Bridge Dead in the Water

JAMES THOMAS STEVENS is the author of five books of poetry, *Tokinish* (First Intensity Press, 1994), *Combing the Snakes from His Hair* (Michigan State UP, 2002), and *(dis)Orient* (Palmpress, 2005), *Mohawk/Samoa: Transmigrations* (Subpress, 2006). *The Mutual Life* (Plan B Press, 2006) and *Bulle/Chimere* (First Intensity, 2006). He is a member of the Akwesasne Mohawk tribe, attended the Institute of American Indian Arts and The Jack Kerouac School of Disembodied Poetics at Naropa and holds an MFA from Brown University.

A Bridge Dead in the Water

James Thomas Stevens

SALT

CAMBRIDGE

PUBLISHED BY SALT PUBLISHING

PO Box 937, Great Wilbraham. Cambridge PDO CB21 5JX United Kingdom

First published 2007

Printed and bound in the United Kingdom by Lightning Source

Typeset in Swift 9.5/13

ISBN 978 1 84471 270 0 paperback

Salt Publishing Ltd gratefully acknowledges
the financial assistance of Arts Council England

for Nicolas

Contents

Introduction

A dead bridge. A dead theory. The Bering Strait theory, dead to Native peoples, whose hundreds of creation accounts dispel those of anthropologists. This collection was written after a trip to China in 2002. After entering the catholic Xujiahui cathedral across from my hotel, I was led to do research on Jesuit interactions with Asia. What I had encountered there in the cathedral and in museums in Shanghai, reminded me of the history of Jesuits back home in Iroquoia, especially in the Mohawk homelands along the Saint Lawrence River.

The first poem in the collection, *(dis)Orient*, addresses issues of charting and mapping, as well as issues of authority. It leads to short poems written in and about China, then on to the central poem, *The Mutual Life*, a poem of post-colonial and personal emergencies. A poem of healing, as well, based on a 1901 book of accidents, emergencies and illnesses published by the Mutual Life Insurance Company of New York. The poems proceeding are poems written in and about Iroquoia.

They are followed by my most recent undertaking, *Alphabets of Letters*, which explores the propaganda found in Native American children's primers from the time of our honored Mohawk chief, Joseph Brant, and the propaganda of rhetoric in general. This poem explores the rhetoric of empire and the short distance our world has moved toward understanding and communication in these past few centuries.

(dis)Orient

*Meaning is revealed by the pattern formed and the light thus trapped—
not by the structure, the carved work itself.*

— W. BION, A Memoir of the Future

*At length all our journeyings, which were made only by paths all strewn
with Crosses, came to an end very fittingly at a lake bearing the name of
the Cross, from it's having the Perfect shape of one.*

— FR. ALBANEL, The Jesuit Relations

How quickly we prescribe

the shape of all things.

In the instant of disorientation,
a dim shimmering
projects uncontainable fear,
spreads out from our wooden boat.

Separation sounds,
soft as wool
pulled from a spindle.

Alone on our glassy seats and rocking,
overcome with need
to chart the waterlight
between
the bow and the border
*with reference to ourselves,
its distance, and what tribes dwell*

on *its shores.*

To place myself
when I have lost you.

Marker.

Born on the shore
of your consequence
though absent
                when you came.

Your desire
to know periphery,
the jagged coast
of your container.

Mapped by echo and story.
A cry returned by crosses
along the strand
does not imply acceptance
of your plan, your shape.

Echo, mirror, story.
Each bent to serve.
Do not listen to me
but yourself listening to me.

What is returned to us,
by recount
or reflection, rendered line.

We obtained all the information we could from the Indians
who had frequented those regions, and we even traced out
from their reports a map of the whole of the new country.

—FR. MARQUETTE, *Recueil de voyages*

You've informed me
of lands where
dark men dance with spades,
their black hair awhirl.

And others, where yellow men
pound winter rivers
that their waters not feel the freeze.
A marble boat
hovers in a vast bright lake

which in my mind
bears your name
for its having the perfect shape
of you.

But how much faith
is required
before making the projection.

Relating your stories,
I feel the irritable reaching,
looking steadily to your experience
till a pattern emerges.

A wind across your surface
and you shiver in every limb.

And I would not
make a rhinoceros of you.

Dürer, how you erred
drawing the creature unseen,
mapping the scaled legs
of the rhino,
his *armoured plates,*
the colour of a speckled tortoise.

An account
of you naked in the gymnasium
before the others. Foreigner.
Your long foreskin
and broad farmer's feet.

If I were to sketch you from your experience...

If the savages are to be believed, in one place, where the birds shed their feathers
at molting time, any Savages or deer coming to the spot are buried in feathers
over their heads, and are often unable to extricate themselves.

—Fr. Albanel, *The Jesuit Relations*

But disregarding your own
savage account of your skin,
I draw you sleeping
            or naked before a mirror.

Buried beneath the down
            of your cruel forearm.

[5]

Supplemented by tales,
all error and conjecture reflected.
I recall your sounding points
as security,
skim your body for meridian.

Surrounded now by minute links
which, impregnated with cruelty,
link your parts together cruelly.

Orient or disorient.
                              Huronia & Cathay.

The landbridge will not be forced
to function
by what you find familiar
                    on either side.

What is *not* familiar around us,
more relevant
                    than what is.

The seduction of delineation,
that mathematically
I might know you,
the circumference of your eye.

The exact length and breadth
of your first finger,
pointing unfailingly
to the sky when you sleep.

Lines that transcend language.

Mathematics & geometry,
a new universe
                of discourse.

*By glancing, as one can, at the Map of the lakes, one will gain more light upon
all these missions than by long descriptions that might be given of them.*

                                        —FR. DABLON, *The Jesuit Relations*

In fear of dislocation
I return to my drawings of you.

Consider my meridian,
neither Paris nor Peking.

No map is a neutral document.

Both in selectivity of content
and sign,
there is bias.

The fine rendering
of a pale blue delta on the your thigh
fades to cool yellow whiteness.

And all that is not you:
the wall, the pillow, the stair,
give way to darkness.
Delicate color disappears.

An atlas of the rivers
on the underside of your foot.

An atlas of the line
where your chest curves to arm.

An atlas
of your open eye.

The many drawings you'll never see.

And my trips
to the liquid parts of you,
more apostolic than geometric...

                           the glistening rim of your mouth.

...where this great lake discharges its waters, is very
advantageous to perform religious
functions, since it is the great resort of most of the
savages of these regions...

Charting by echo
of sense, both thought and real.

Compelled to seek asylum in fiction,
because disguised as fiction, the truth occasionally slips through.

But whose truth, whose meridian
would show your proper placement?

Not wanting to move you away
by either idolatry or insult.

When seeing yourself so large,
myself in a distant corner,
or sometimes drawn so small,
you are lost in the warm port beneath my arm.

...the more ignorant began to make fun of such a description but
the more intelligent, seeing such an orderly arrangement of
parallel lines of latitude and longitude ... could not resist believing
the whole thing true.

—FR. RICCI, Lettres Edifiantes et Curieuses des Jesuites de Chine

Born between inland seas,
I travel toward water's
                    empirical truth.
The roiling glass reflection.

Show me how I've acted, looked, done.
Give to me.

Water formed borders,
the silk city of Suzhou,
carved from lakebed,
                    contained by canal.
Echo.

The other returns to us
unthinkable dread,
projected through reverie,
                    in bearable form.

The sound of the oar returned
by the tiled roofs of Han Shan Sì
or here,
the loon's cry, resounding
from painted rocks beside the Sault.

> It is that beauty which is nothing but the beginnings of terror
> that we are still just able to bear...

My native mind,
orientalists say,

    ...more concerned with what happened at the
place than
      the place itself. The route represented as
continuous line.

The symbols similar
on both sides of the sea,

> *While skirting some frightfully huge rocks, we saw upon one of them
> two monsters painted there that startled us at first. Even the boldest
> Indians dare not rest their eyes on them for long. They are as large as
> a calf, with horns on their heads like those of deer, a horrible look,
> red eyes, a beard like a tiger, a face somewhat like a man's, a body
> covered with scales and a long tail that encircles the body, passing
> above the head and going back between the legs, ending in a fish's
> tail. These two monsters were so well painted that we could not believe
> that they were executed by a savage.*
>
>   —Fr. Marquette, *Recueil de voyages*

Our margins of comfort
might be marked
with nameless terror

or inscribed on the rocks,
the sign of your narrow hips,
signaling
    safe passage.

[13]

Last night, my face beneath
the light framework of your knee.

Night anchorage
at Maple bridge
or the matrix of bodily awareness.

Locate me.

A bat
etched into a charred canyon wall,
or carved on a beam above
the canal's east gate,

is an empathetic creature.

Charting solely by
what is returned.

Each image projected
through my experience of you,
with you,
bounced off your bias and
tender aesthetic.

No concept of felt objects,
the shoreline shifts with travel.

And the space does fill
with what it is that's happened.

Experience overcomes exactitude,
all scale is lost.
The canoe or ship
appearing bigger than the sea.
Your warm hand larger than the hills.

The lakes laid to line
   for missionary zeal,
     ...influenced by a most ardent desire to make him *known*
     and adored by all peoples of all countries.

Lacus Huronum et Tai Hu.

Aware of the empirical
and angered by infidels, who blur all distinction
between actual, lived space and imaginary, idealized space.

Not above adding soft folding hills
below an auspicious ridge,
to create a more favorable
               geomantic space.

Linking the lived to the imagined,
I recall only the silent pause
between harsh words—the reconciliation
not the wronging.

Wanting
to avoid
    the empty space.

He moves in and fills the room
with familiar objects.

Lying beneath a pine,
in the damp scent of red needles,
a white bough bends
               over me.

The senses ring familiar
and I hang
pictures of you and I
    across the hostile void.

Then comfort comes in recognition.

The little people who inhabit these shifting tenements, strike camp in the morning all together, to go fishing or work in the rice; they sow and they gather here three times a year...One might say they are ready to embrace [our religion]; but he would be mistaken. They respond coldly: Your religion is nowhere in our books, it is a strange religion...

—FR. DE PRÉMARE, *Lettres Edifiantes et Curieuses des Jesuites de Chine*

The Indians gather and prepare [the rice] for food as follows. In the month of September, which is the proper time for the harvest, they go in canoes through these fields of wild rice and shake its ears into the canoe...I told these Wild Rice People of my design to go and discover remote nations in order to teach them the mysteries of our holy religion...They told me that I would meet nations who never show mercy to strangers, but break their heads for no reason...

—FR. MARQUETTE, *Recueil de voyages*

What I tell you is
      what I want to hear,
but the words are dull,
      a mouthful of rice.

No making opposite shores connect,
the landbridge dead in the water.

If I name the rapid—La Chine
      it does not bring China closer.

As stroking the rough skin of
the pine above me,
      does not make it yours.

My fingers through your hair.
Needles.

And the coast shifts regardless
of our desire
for things to remain the same.

The pines now replaced
            by silos and stacks.

An image of you
constructed, but never abandoned.

From the boat, from a distance,
so simple to assume quietude.
Calm points
            of placement along the shore,
despite the maddening clang of tin
from elevators along a canal.

And from water's edge
the boat assumed silent, though
the deafening clap
of wind through skins from the mast
            both fore and aft.

Confused by what
is returned from what was imagined.

Lost in the roar that exists
            on the other side of silence.

Three Translations from Characters Found on a Lover's Body

I.

The earth and its foregoing, this could be horizon.
Combined, the radicals pressed into one another.
What do we represent lying held in men and arms,
to erect gold and sun and legs (running)?
I call you disc, sun entangled in the branches of a tree.
Rice field over struggle, earth over self.
Effacement. Your mouth is a carriage
and the carriage plus the tenth of a cubit is turn,
bent knuckle revolving around a pivot.
Common, is the object beneath the bench.
Plant, covers, knife, a weed
extended to mean govern, the flame in the middle
of the lamp is the man with ample arms,
blend and pace in the midst of court.
Your torso sings Garden.   Composes.

II.

Mastery of weeds extends to mean:
plants blending to cover the middle of lamp.
A knife for a flame, foregoing the earth,
this is the horizon of a man with arms.
To move across your body, I am the carriage
and the cubit, the disc running tangled
in the branches of a tree.
I am the common object beneath the bench,
the wheel running length
of the rutted road
down to the garden of abdomen.
I struggle over fields
to kiss a mouth filled with rice,
to put away evil.   This is earth over self.

III.

Beneath a table of common struggles
I blend and pace in ample arms.
A rice field foregoing garden
on the horizon of your belly.
Govern the revolving cubit, the bent knuckle.
Me over you, over self, a tree.
Earth entangled in the branches of a knife.
Plant and cover inside your mouth,
the turning disc,
the carriage and wheel.
To erect lamps in the bend
of your gold leg running
is to extend the word
to mean master, garden or weed.

Five Poems from the Paintings of Lang Shining

(Italian Jesuit Painter—Giuseppe Castiglione)

Eight Horses

The half light breeds shadows
        beneath the feathered willow.
A half breed lights
        on the plain of your chest.

And Lang Shining
who I consider a kind
            of brother-in-law,
did he know nights?

Like the one before we rode
the treachery of travel.

You in the shadow of
the nation's exploding
        and exploited blossoms,
me in San Francisco's misty green
                and green
but I'm blue for lack of your hand.

Did he know of the night before,
        when like the grey cloaked groomer
pressed small against
        a chalk white steed,
I felt the gallop
        of a thousand horses
where you lay gasping
            across my back.

Dog Under Flowers

Jealous little glare
of Shining's dog beneath
                    the bone tree.
Erotic ossicles, like
        weaving through
the framework
        of your solid knee.
Lovely bone
that sets your legs so beautifully
where you stand
                    above me.

Your firm naked feet on the ground.

You are on my mind today
under citrus limbs
                in the Mission,
where I found my way back
by the dense scent of
                    blossoms.

Bad little dog
        in a splay pawed stance.

On returning I seek
the smell
        of your skin
which despite my jealousy,
        plants beauty in my head.

The White Gibbon

Dark Dunkirk again,
naked for the first full night
this spring.
The air finally allowing for
the long drag
from whiskered jawline
      to whispered toe.

And a white monkey wakes
unfurling his tail
along the inside of my arm.

We hear the watery stir
of stars
making their way
          across Erie.

Who painted this monkey
here against my heart,
his wide eyes alert
to the birds you've forced
      from winter's branches,
but frenetically picking
      the pricking little angers
from hairs matted down
by a rainstorm
      across your thigh.

Pheasants Among Rocks and Flowers

Leaves hang heavy
        this morning.
Plumed birds plucked
for the heads of white clouds.
See Catlin
        for the connection.
Maybe you were right
        about the land bridge,
about it all.

The way Shining's
fiery feathers disappeared
over the sea,
the pale blue of his stones
played out in the Ioway sky.

White Cloud
with his round head,
a hand
        over his mouth,
it comes together.

The ease
        with which
your tongue becomes
mine.

And when you whisper
Wo xiang ni,

Wo ye hen xiang ni,
hums
        in my painted mouth.

The Time-Telling Plant from the West

Late afternoon—
the full sun, returning
naked from the kitchen
        to find you
closed and perpendicular
to the bruised line
                of lakeshore.
Relieved and smaller
than when I left,
the small hairs sensitive
to the air as I enter.

I want to write
across your gorgeous thigh
as Qianlong scrawled
across the exquisite faces
                of paintings.
Black lines over
the rise of your hip
        descending
                to minutia.
Perfect ideograms
                inside your navel.

Alert the guards
that I am stealing
from the emperor's hand,
transcribing
        to your thigh
his well thought lines:

When touched it goes to sleep, then it wakes. Rare things ought not be
praised, but this is strange and deserves a poem.

Remembering Shanghai: 3 Poems

Bianfú

From the glass lobby of the Jianguo Hotel
I watch a blue plastic river, peddle by in the mist,
occasionally the daring traveler sporting red,
or a yellow hood on converging currents.
All day considering rivers, their effect on desire.

Overwhelming rain. Overwhelming reflection.
Too ancient & neon. Turning
to the gift shop, behind more glass, an orange orb
of carved Qing Tian stone, an orgy of
bats and peaches. A warm orange glow despite
the rain and grey clatter of bicycles.

Peach and bat. The unexpected juxtaposition.
The too obvious cleave on the peach's curved
edge, begs for contemplation of the fine down
at the base of a spine, the warm rounded halves
of any part and every parcel of pleasure.

This morning, I'm handed a rough short story by a
polished boy, the sort who can manage a type of ascot.
Blue silk round the neck like a rakish Frenchman.
I read: *I take off my clothes at the sinking sun.*
I turn, belly up, floating in the lake.
Bats dive at me, pull back, scream and dive again.

How quickly the incongruous comes to clarity.
That a bat would be drawn to the belly of youth,
the taut curve divided, the downy line.
Wings spread wide against bare broad shoulders.

In my age things are changing, becoming more
touching. I can cry at the perfect *shoe-ness* of a
beautiful boy's brown shoe.
And when I see him with the silk bat sucking
at his long neck, I wish only
that he have good fortune and a long life.

Xishuài

Bushes toss at the iron gatehouse.
There is a racetrack, colonial
(Oh those Brits) beneath the grass.
Renmin Gongyuan/People's Park
is one hundred and thirteen
degrees by calculation. A cricket
chirps seventy three times
in fifteen seconds, add forty. It is
one hundred and thirteen degrees.

His black legs, otherworldly smooth
to the naked eye. Burnished steel.
Black antithesis to the white legs of
men at the edge of this pond, beneath
a clock tower—early British modern.

In the park there is a pond. There is
a racetrack beneath the broad feet
of fisherman. Shanghai Race Course
circling endlessly under koi. At
the edge of the pond there are crickets.
Men step from brown water. Reflections
of an enormous golden carp
spewing rope light.

And there is nothing so beautiful,
causing such song,
as the dull thudding reverberation
of a man's firm ankle placed hard
on stone at the edge of a pool.
Muscle tremulous

for one resonant moment.

I think of this today
where you step from clear water
into your blue foam sandal.
So blue that I can only understand it
as the opposite of China.

Lóng

Whispers through the vegetarian
dining hall stop a tardy monk on
his golden-robed way. Plastic forks
drop. *Lóng* has reappeared.
It is spring at Longhua temple,
cradle of the colour yellow.

Smoke from etched bronze censers
winds with the late winds
around the pagoda. On the
stone steps beside me, five long toes, long
as fingers, on a wooden sandal
reach from beneath the
belled-bottom of his jeans.

I try to make out the nine resemblances;
head of a camel, horns of a deer, eyes
of a rabbit, etc. Not there, but beneath
the edge of his hard jaw I glimpse
one bright pearl. *Lóng*, it's spring and
your five toes show an imperial line.

Purple shirted street thug
shrugging whiskery strands from rabbit
eyes. You take one long draw on your
last cigarette, virility streaming
from your bactrian nose.

I wonder at the number of scales
armouring your heart—81 yang
line the ridge of your left ventricle.

36 yin on the right, allow for beauty.

But the rains come and you're gone
beneath a tiled gate,
leaving just hints
of your glistening scales
in the bark of a rain-swept pine.

Canal

The Emperor, Qianlong ordered a celebration for his mother's 50th birthday.
As the water route from the Peking Palace to Yuan Ming Yuan was frozen
solid, thousands of workers were charged with beating the water day and
night to prevent ice from forming. This proved fruitless.

—*Lettres édifiantes,* vol. 23

Now the green beginnings of the peach
hang from a Chinese branch. Hard little fists
shaking at spring in the summer palace,
somewhere here beneath a sternum
sore with working new earth.

This river, is it the wanting, too well known?
From the southern temple, where I
am all body, touch and scent? This canal
to the red tiled palace, locus, they say of love's
innocuous little barge. Who located the heart
so high, in generous oversight?

And who do I employ for the beating of these veins?
Where canals freeze between the stone banks of
blank familiarity and small arguments that harden—
layer on layer.

There are secrets they say, to maintaining
flow. Fluids that move us to celebration
beneath the gates. In the backyard, gorges of blossoms
hang from two species of pear tree, spreading scent,
a strange sweet mingling of warm feet and perfumes.

I am digging and it feels like work
to keep the balance, the shovel's repetitive blow.
And startled, a sulfur-gold oriole rises

from the overturned earth in endless furrow,
and it occurs to me to question the reverse.

Of waters become too liquid, where other springs resurge
strong.
Floods drip-strangle the garden of perfect brightness,
where hydrous arms reach beyond their well-worn beds.
How to harden superfluid desire?
If emperor, I'd order a million red troupes
to press their thick fingers to this gushing in my heart.

The Mutual Life

.

Relationships, Colonization
And Other Accidents

A Manual for Reference

Section I.

Accidents

A policy may not prevent an accident,
but it will materially aid in recovery.

I thought of painting you last night.
The tragic/edy
of it all, contending.
A bystander's lack of knowledge
as to what should be
or has been done. The colors.

The disposition to rely on
cumbrous instruments,
circumstantially hurtful or
utterly mean. To see
what has happened
in the hues of my own choosing.

What happened there, arboreal,
up for discussion. Knocked
to my hands and knees. Knee-knocked.
Omit the technical terms.

Just respectfully suggesting
scientific terms be remembered
beneath the loins.
Clothed behind popular expressions.

In one place
meaning one thing, two.
Or nothing at all.

Shock.

Of seeing through a new eye.
The new color, mandate. Learning
life may be destroyed by certain   agencies.
A blow to the pit, (ash or other)
certain ashes clinging to a basket.

Or a sudden emotion of the mind, comet,
or flying head, hailstone,
caress of foot, no trace be left
in any part of the   body.

Pallor of the patient
in utter prostration. The folds of
your long skin, pallid
where the moccasin puckers.   *Otsipwe.*

Treatment.–This consists
of gentle friction to red extrem(ists)ities.
The aromatic character of brandy
will not be rejected.

I was pushed against a tree.
He struck the blow. I am more than one,
repeated blows by removal. Forcing
ice chips inside me, split from the thin edge
with the point of a pin.

Flannels wrung out in hot (pox blankets)
water should not be neglected.
Seems a revival of the action
of the heart, enough brandy has been given.

Asphyxia.

Of which several varieties: (1)
due to submersion, as in
ordinary, water or other fluids.

Strange submersion in our own
cont(inents)ainers. Otherly white fluid arms
pressing pulse. Appealing to venous
where arterial wants invocation.

A body dies, because blood is not purified;

(2)
from mechanical causes
strangling or the gallows.

1862
thirty-eight choking
the collective throat. Gagged.
Reflexive.   *Mdewakanton.*

Foreign body hanging
in the windpipe or approaches;

(3)
from torpor of
the medulla oblongata.
Thirty seven snap in time.
One needing to be restrung.

See: Treatment.—

Artificial respiration.

After the artifice, impurities
so far removed, allow
for a natural breathing.

The newly natural.
How to paint the historiscape—
your tongue pulled forward to
favor passage. Drawing arms
away and upward.
Language, by means
of which the ribs are raised,
I want you inside me.

A smoking windpipe beside the fire.

Arms laid down
on the pit of your white belly.

Something quite difficult
to keep the tongue from slipping backward,
a word pulling back
into its thinly-voweled wimple.

If language is too slippery,
a hatpin, hairpin or paintbrush
may be passed right through. The colors
across my tongue from drawing
the brush between pursed lips. Purse-lips. Cowslip. Your little
        lips bruised.

Turn the body once more
on its face, gentle pressure used to the back.

Accidents from Lightning.

When the body is rendered
in oils, or unconscious,
clothing should be rapidly removed.
A bed, warmth applied
especially to the pit,
certain ashes smeared in your burden basket.

And brandy.

Burns and Scalds.

When clothing catches fire in the park or dew
of nocturnal parking above the falls (I'd
seen them a thousand times but
when he saw them, they were discovered).
Beneath the windshield, his fingers fanned out
above the bush.
The burn, superficial
as far as depth is concerned,
but his white hand hovering considered
more serious, than a burn, smaller, deeper
but more complete.

Treatment.—
Sweet oil alone is very good;
whereas wheaten flour, with the discharge,
hardens.
Small comfort, as if small loaves of bread
(fish) were applied to the injured part.

In shock and depression, brandy or whiskey.

Note.—
Scalds are more confined to the skin, unless
the burning element doesn't rapidly run off
(with) the part which it came in.   Contact.

Contusions.

How common the pushing,
my knees in eastern leaves.
In the simple form only   a shaking
(as of rattles turtle-shell gourd or bone antler)
or jarring of the texture
with no visible change but a rupture
                          of the vessel.
In severe form, parts to pulp.
Gourds along the roadside, privates meat
and flies.

The quantity of blood (skins) escaping
depending on the size
and number of broken vessels. Ship wreck. Run aground.
        Contretemps. Ram.
Our fortune in collision
when the vessel cracked. The button unbutton and whistling
        zipper.
A single vessel divided,
split on scalp, allows a (sea) swelling.
The looseness of tissues.

Discoloration of a continent
indicating intense injury.
Dark blue, crimson, down to delicate pink.

In the window, twinned tight amaryllis buds, their smooth-
                grooved undersides.
  Two perfect burning scarlet whales poised beneath your
              white keel.

Elevate, if possible, these parts above your heart.

Fractures.

There is always some shock
and great pain.

A hank of daffodils newly snapped,
dripping like a youth
who finds for the first time
                              another's hand
against his open thigh.

Hands alert
amid the stillness of their palms.

Therefore never lift a man
till you have satisfied yourself

as to the presence   or   absence

                              of his fracture.

Dislocations.

Relocation.
You saw that coming.
                      We didn't.

Wounds.

So much red and red, the raw
canvas snagged
on the edge of the stretcher.

Incised.   Punctured.   Contused.   Lacerated.   Poisoned.

When the wound is extensive
the shock is profound.

Redpaint pots found in excavation,
our own carefully incised along its fluted edge.

Millions of tiny mouths spilling their stories.

All that we can do, is aid nature in the process,
making the mouths of the vessels
                                                    ever smaller
through pressure, a firm hand
against the artery by which their stories flow.

Pressure best applied
to the stories, the pulsations
     of which can be felt.

Stories in the lower extremities.

Poor John Smith
his story felt   —   pulsating
about the middle of the groin.

Backward against bone
between fingers and thumb
                    applied.

While one person is doing this,
another can tie in a handker-
chief
a small stone or piece of wood,
a watch or anything hard.

Slip a stick through
the knot twisting
till the story stops flowing.

     ~

If an artery in the scalp is cut, firm pressure over the wound will
always control the dream. It is well to remember in great emer-
gency, nearly any dreaming can be checked for a time by thrust-
ing a finger into the wound and pressing directly on the
dreaming point.

Layers of flexible collodian across the scalp
help to remind of the reality of rifles (see: External Remedies)

Collodian.

This is a solution of gun-cotton in alcohol and ether, with a little
castor oil to make the mixture flexible. The alcohol and ether
evaporate in a few seconds, leaving a firm flexible film closely
applied to the mind.

Do we have a palette yet?

My narrative captured
            in plaster or paint.

The next step is dressing
or undressing   his wound.

Place strips closely
across the lines of trauma,
taking care that our edges
            are brought close together.

1877   *Tsitsistas.*
Twenty-two exiled,
their broad bones cast in
plaster (see: Mills, Clark—American sculptor).

Wolf's Marrow. Long Back. White Man. Left Hand. Shaving Wolf.

…when we take it off we expect to find the wound healed.

My red forehead pressed hard
beneath your white belly.

Bites of Dogs.

All dogs will bite, once over the   water.
                              (fear of)

Destiny manifest itself under two forms:

1. In furious form, an augmented activity of locomotives, a disposition to bite upon quitting the bark.

2. In sullen form, shyness and depression; no desire to bite back; melancholy; general depression of the spirits; although he fears no fluids, he does not drink.

Treatment.—Remove the clothing, if any, from the bitten part.

Section II.

Emergencies

As a preparation for emergencies, there can be
nothing better than a policy in THE MUTUAL LIFE.

Earache.

Tenderness, a dangerous
smoking signal
          behind the ear
of serious mischief in your
          under/lying
structure.

You speak or don't. Hand signals. Sign language. A nipple
between thumb & forefinger.

        Linen scrap in laudanum
        cut into bits
        place in the bowl of a tobacco pipe
        light it
        cover it
        insert the stem (mouthpiece)
        so as not to hurt
        into the ear
        apply the lips to the bowl
        blowing smoke
        of burning opium
        inside the ear.

Toothache.

Your heated fig held inside. Promise.

Faceache.

Neuralgic quincentennial.
A heated hop-pillow and ordinary stiff
red paste
of Indian-meal and honey.

Croup.

The well-known hoarseness
coming on hard at night
always the possibility of an attack by the croup.

Counting coup. Plenty Coup. Cooing, insistent inside your
hot ear.

Foreign Bodies in the Eye.

Generally dislodged,
washed out by tears
due to someone's irritation
           but sometimes
                necessary to resort to extraction.

Should the foreign body be imbedded, east of the river's membrane,
a steady hand and rigid instrument will usually lift it out, clearing
the horizon for the sun to set behind your western shoulder.

Foreign Bodies in Nostrils and Ear.

The curious disposition   — at sixteen —
of children
to insert foreign bodies;

as grains of coffee, corn, a finger, peas, pebbles, once, your little
toe in my nose.

If the body is soft, absorbing moisture,
you become swollen/sullen—more difficult to remove
from this tract, developing
into a life.

If the body is hard, inflammation fanning
fires by your lodges at night,
your irritation increases   — my desire to move.

Poison Vine Eruption.

Swamp sumach.
Poison oak.
Fruit of knowledge.
Poison sumach.
Poison vine.

I found there was a new nakedness under your skin.

Treatment.— Powder the globe liberally with exfoliant. Weakened
lead-water is also recommended.

Sunstroke.

I fainted when you arrived at my door, with that bouquet of fluorocarbons. Thankfully, our neighbour now has a bathtub large enough to hold an entire body.

Immerse me entirely.
Put an ice-cap on my head.

Frostbite.

> Steal cattle if you're cold
> and rub my blue parts
> with beef-tea.

Convulsions.

Sometimes a general convulsion
of a continent,   sometimes parts of it only.
At first the face is pale
then livid except,
                     around the mouth
which often continues pale.

You said: *Diné, Lakota, Inuit, Hochunk, Tohono O'otam, Tsalagi,
Anishnaabe...*
You say: Navajo, Sioux, Eskimo, Winnebago, Papago, Cherokee,
Chippewa...

An attack might only last five minutes, but to bystanders it
naturally seems longer.

Attacking the canvas,
you emerge
from a flap, from colour—a purplish tint
       where your moccasin

                    puckers.
Your broad farmer's feet
slip
                on tanned hides.

Still this morbid fasci/nation with your zinc white skin.

Cholera Morbus.

A disease due entirely
to eating poisonous foods.

Symptomatic— a marked prostration, a going
to the knees, to the chantry on the point.

Hot black robes applied,
to the abdomen. Nothing given
by mouth
         at first.

But you are the guest
of progress,
your host is on your tongue.

        Unhappy apostates, forced to *His* marble feet.

Malaria.

Our stories hardened
as veins of flint.   *Kanienkehaka.*

At first only two
mosquitoes,
of the river,
warriors
Moving to
moved course.
pouncing and
and heads.
shoulders slung
clubs on their belts.
with many arrows,
their canoes, that
fight the creatures on
their death songs
And the creatures
Men tore their
from their blood
little mosquitoes,
with them, angry for
of their grandfathers.

great ones,
one on each side
spearing 5 or many
with their large beaks.
other rivers as men
Taking more men,
devouring hands
20 warriors, 2 canoes,
with bows. War
Filled the air
half killed in
those left could
land, singing
as they went.
fell to the earth.
bodies to bits, and
flew millions of
the air soon full
the slaughter
Hungry for
blood.

To prevent development—do not go out after sunset,
nor near freshly plowed land.

Your home should not be

in a hollow
and your bedroom above
my head or higher.

I don't hate you for the death of my grandfathers, though I may
blame you now and then for the red bumps in the road, the
quinine and the gin.

Section III.

Poisons

The effect of the accidental administration of poison may be greatly mitigated by a policy in THE MUTUAL LIFE.

Poisons.

There is not a single person
on the entire list,
who may not be used
to advance
          another's body.

Likewise, scarcely
a single one indulged in
beyond the requirements
          of the body
that may not be followed
by a derangement of the economy.

We are not miscalled
if all called   —   Poisons.

    Bring me up with ipecacuanha, mustard, zinc, milk white,
        feather inside your throat.
    I'll bring you up with common salt. The sea on which you
        came.

Poisoning by Mushrooms.

Once enticed, you take
the perfect mushroom
      on your tongue.

false morels ~ *gyromitra* ~ your spinning head ~ green spored
lepiota ~ *chlorophyllum molybdites* ~ a dusting on the bulb ~
destroying angel ~ *amanita virosa* ~ red faces pocked with
white.

Spores break free, spew across the land. A mushroom's cloud
above your desert home.

Poisonous Meats

      Federal standard: PCB's 3 parts per million for foul.

Poisonous Fish

2 parts per million.

Reservation. Preservation. A male turtle caught at a northern
reserve read
3,067 parts per million, qualified to be classified, toxic waste.
His female counterpart, able to shed her own contamination by
laying eggs,
835 parts per million.

Mineral Poisons

How to paint this, let me count the ways. A peculiar train of
symptoms. A painters' colic.

AMMONIA.

ALIZARINE ORANGE.

ANTIMONY.

ARSENIC.

BARYTA.

CADMIUM RED.

COBALT BLUE.

COPPER.

DIOXAZINE PURPLE.

IODINE.

IRON.

LEAD.

LIME.

MANGANESE BLUE.

MERCURY.

NICKEL TITANIUM YELLOW.

PHOSPHORUS.

POTASH.

SILVER.

TIN.

TITANIUM WHITE.

ZINC WHITE.

Vegetable Poisons

The vegetable earth on its mineral spine.

Section IV.

Remedies

Next in value to the prevention of disease or
accident is indemnity for the possible results
of both. THE MUTUAL LIFE provides such indemnity

I decided last night
to paint you in poisons,
Vermeer-concise
          in my conceit.

But your body,
wouldn't stop
        suggesting precious metaphors.

Remembering how continents
clashed in the night,
the scar on your abdomen
marked by a whiter whiteness,
        whispered   history.

Our portrait, a thin red line in a field of white.

The soft palette sore from the remedy.

Notes

Otsipwe—Ojibwa or Chippewa; from the Algonquin for "puckered", referring to their moccasin style. p. 3.

Mdewakanton—A band of Dakota people; from the Dakota *mde*—lake and *wakan*—sacred mystery. p. 4.

Tsitsistas—Cheyenne; poss. from the Cheyenne for "people who look like this" or "people who come from over there." p. 11.

Kanienkehaka—Mohawk; from the Mohawk for "people of the flint." p. 17.

A Species of Martyrdom:
The Huronia Series

Jean de Brébeuf (d. March 16, 1649)
St. Ignace, Ontario

To kiss the stake
    one's bound to

fall to erotic postures.

And isn't this like
the burning below the navel?

                  A fiery belt of pitch.

I recognize in it
        a hatchet-headed collar
and a molten red rising
    from the pitcher of your throat.

Like a ceremony of scalding
to know the first
      little death
of the one beside you,
          realizing
that bound hands don't
by necessity
      mean prayer.

Gabriel Lalemant (d. March 17, 1649)
St. Ignace, Ontario

And the larger death you chose

to stay
the entire course.

Unsuspecting of outliving.

Yes, for the long haul.

But when the other head droops
like a chrysanthemum
                on a catafalque,
you're left to endure
                the song of other birds,

soothed only by the painful prick
of your knees
                on the forest floor.

Anthony Daniel (d. July 4, 1648)
Ihonatiria Mission, Ontario

Whatever you imagined
                    in the air,
invisible and without body
        no worse than what was.

Entering like a span of sparrows,
the dove
aligned with the virgin's loins.

And the news is clear.

That this body would be flung
into the fires
                    of its mission,
to love the unlovable
                    and bring them home.

René Goupil (d. September 23, 1642)
Andagaron, New York

You made the sign
     and how human it suddenly felt
when the last nail slipped
        from your finger,
the last finger gnawed
        from its knuckle.

He took your broken
           face in hand
applying words
     to wounds,
            He hath no form nor comeliness...
When they hatcheted
your fine head aflame
       with god,
he weighted you under
        waters.

And when they dragged you
to mulch
     in the moldering leaves,
he sought your skull
and lifting it to his lips,
noted
     the tiny rattle of ecstasy.

Jean de Lalande (d. October 19, 1646)
Ossernenon, New York

Now I tender my congratulations
because I've offered once (or twice)
to be that man.

But you made it to the end
and still
        by his side,
suffered blows
        and stinging limbs.

I wanted
to see someone through

but in the end
        when their heads fell like berries
from rain swollen stakes,
I had already been retired from
                those passionless fields,
farmed out to another
        before the fall.

Isaac Jogues (d. October 18, 1646)
Ossernenon, New York

So often the wounds
make life
            canonically impossible,
but granted privilege
to perform
            despite them,
you were loved doubly—

two coveting your side in death.

And when stripped
of your thumb
like a green branch drawn
and twisted
            from its unyielding skin,

Patience was your physician.

Your head beside his,
on the palisade not the pillow,
watching
your own pale arms and legs
spin pinwheel
                down the river.

Charles Garnier (d. December 7, 1649)
St. Jean Village, Ontario

Lamb to the lion,
your frail frame
            miraculously resisting.

How awesome the strength of the tongue
to trick them to fraternity.

No stopping your scuttling,
your hastening toward the stake
            to baptize and exhort.

But when the Tobacco fell
in rows around you
and a heat bird flew
            through your shoulder,
how short-lived
            absolution.

A blow to the very act of charity.

Noël Chabanel (d. December 8, 1649)
Nottawasaga River, Ontario

Grapes frozen beneath a blanket
of snow along the bay.

No heavy juice dripping
on the soil of
your Huron vineyard.

Oh bloodless martyr in the shadow of martyrdom.

No Huron trickles
from your heavy French tongue.

And your martyrdom, not due to death,
but the sentence of living
                    a life so indelicate.

Removed from missions
so fertile in palms and crowns,
till mercifully the apostate
crushed your sweet grape to wine.

Scarlet stains on the ice floe
                    fade to orange.

The sweetest berry saved till last.

Pax

Sickened by discount lilies beneath florescent lights
or last night's wine, their sweet trumpets drooping;
the cashier, unhappy to have risen so early this easter,
made no special note of this man buying mouthwash.

I recognized in his green eyes and the unhappy turn of
his cheekbone, mixed blood, some dried along his fingers.
And he lifted his chin toward the dim symphony of
supermarket speakers, acknowledging me as a brother.

The cashier laughed at the sheet-marks on his cheek
but they were lines pressed hard from his concrete bed,
a dewy web dangling from his downy brown ear.
Suddenly touching, that he might worry about his breath.

Strange puzzle of a wordless man buying mouthwash.
Then it hits me that it's sunday on these pentacostal plains,
liquor stores closed. No dreams for a day—or too many
to endure. The sunday service offers wine, but for a price.

So I drove concentric circles, wanting nothing more than to
prove myself wrong, or hold him through the tremors
if I found myself right. But there by a rushing storm-drain,
the plastic bottle passed hands in his swaying congregation.

And if I could, I would have pressed him so tightly
that between us, we'd form one perfect sober man
and let the pale drunk sleep away his sheepish dreams.

Lacrosse Night—Iroquoia

Because the boys are brown
or at very least golden,
I have come
to watch
this turn of wrist
        red and smooth,
twist within the webbing
a hard truth
        that could smash
two dark lips red
or leave a cold ear stinging.

Passing shirtless
but for shoulder pads,
he shakes
        the sharp black points
of his hair.
Sting of sweat
on the back of my hand.

My brother,
ten years younger and infinitely kinder,
touches my arm
        with four words,
That player is mean.

He's playing the game, I say.
I don't look
        at my brother
when I answer,
for tonight I've seen

in angry muscle,
a familiar tremour.

And when we leave the arena
crossing Cattaraugus Creek,
there are fires beneath the bridge,
jacklights,
attracting mean designs
to hang themselves neatly
on a row of shining hooks.

Tonawanda Swamps

As it would for a prow, the basin parts with your foot.
Never a marsh, of heron blue
                                    but the single red feather
from the wing of some black bird, somewhere
a planked path winds above water,
the line of sky above this aching space.

Movement against the surface
is the page that accepts no ink.
A line running even
over alternating depths, organisms, algae,
a rotting leaf.

Walk naked before me
carrying a sheaf of sticks.
It's the most honest thing a man can do.

As water would to accept you,
I part
a mouth, a marsh, or margin
is of containment,
the inside circuitous edge.

No line to follow out to ocean,
no river against an envelope
                                    of trembling white ships.
Here I am landlock.
Give me your hand.

Pan-Am

for M.M.

Walking the expo grounds
one hundred years too late, the city of lights
is redundant, because you speak the character—*denghuo*
and it hangs there in the park, where
for years Buffalo has bumped its endless
knee in blackness.

Two buildings remain in imitation grandeur at the
end of the lake, above the bubbling of mud turtles.
A rotten carp floats at the feet of Art and History.

And in the museum, glass cases fan out
from a radial spot in The Gallery of Small Objects.
Behind a wall, semi-circular room,
Chou-ting — the bronze tripod is etched
on it's subtle green incurvature
and I ask you to read to me, plunging
into that thicket of calligraphy.

Man.   There is the symbol for man.
Quan.   Dog.
Sickle.   This thing for cutting grass.

Your head is low and close to mine,
but we can not make out
the writing below the neck of the *Chou-ting*.

And I look at your unshaven face to find
the character for desire. Fine wisps written
above your red open collar.
Sadly, I can't read Chinese and the symbols I seek
are likely hidden in dark periphery.

Later looking into the window
of an antique store, I tell you, I was bored
one day so I built a cricket cage.
And you say, That's like saying I was bored
one day so I wrote a novel. You laugh
when you say this and in it I hear
three species of maple supporting the wind.

The Awful Ease of Tides

for Arthur Sze

I.

Somehow precise and unquestionable,
the cut of the Chinese man's hair.
Never before this certainty,
I consider the decision of each strand.
The diameter. The angle.
So black, the way it appears,
crashing against the hard corner of his jaw.

II.

I consider the darkness.
You are appointed court photographer. Consider this picture.

III.

My small face is red behind a bath towel curtain.
I watch a funeral that is taking place next door.
So black, my dog,
hurling himself against a chain link fence.

IV.

The casket is lowered and I am removing rusty pins
from the grease on the window's aluminum track,
along with strands of hair.

V.

This is pressing.
I mark it with an asterisk. Black and large.

VI.

A vague feeling,
pressing itself against a snowfence in my mind.
Like a threat, I view the way you cut your hair.
as if it were a history of something small.

ALPHABETS OF LETTERS

or

A

NEW

PRIMER

For The

USE of NATIVE or CONFUSED
AMERICANS.

by

JAMES THOMAS STEVENS

for Th. Sgro

A PRIMER for the USE of MOHAWK CHILDREN

Alphabets of Letters.

Vowels.

a e i o u.

Vowels.

A E I O U.

Roman.

1   2   3   4   5

a b c, d e f, g h i, j k l, m n o,

6   7   8   9

p q r, ſs t, u v w, x y z.

A B C, D E F, G H I, J K L,

M N O, P Q R, S T U, V W X, Y Z.

The Alphabet out of Order.

B R C D G X T L Z N V Y I J M W H K E F A
U S O Q P.

It will never be the same.
The alphabet out of order,
your tongue
in mandate direction.

Shatikwáthos *tsi* *nón:we* *nihatí:teron.*
*Tenhsh***theyontátk***meeten'* *iá:ken'* *ne*
*rona***theytenro'shó***friends***n:'a* *ne* original
people*nkwehonwé:ke kwáh she's iá:*it is said*ken'* could
not*iáh tha'*speak a *taonta*word*hontá:ti' ne onkw*of the way
*ehon*of the original*wehné*people*ha'.* Silence.

Have you learned it yet?
Let me teach you the new word for *you.*
Let us teach them the new word for *themselves.*

[85]

**A Conſonant can make no sound or Syllable
without a Vowel either before or after it.**

I   alone was a consonant
waiting for you to school me.

School us.

Your primers across or drifting down
from godly superfine blue. Nothing
in print is a neutral document.
Your rhetoric, dim and thinning
for 500 years.

Primers from London's royal lot
to warn her brown children of Popiſh plots.

Brant, lettered Chief,
you foresaw the missionary meltdown,
understood the alphabet
as more than religious creed. Land. Oil. Gold. Labour.

I.   gad   tad   gag   7.

Bab		wad	lag		Lift	Sift	boʃs	Holm	poʃt
cab	2.		mag	ling	ʃing	bolt	hone	plot	
dab	Had	3.	pag	link	ʃign	blot	hogs	prop	
gab	jad	Bag	nag	lick	ʃigh	Cobs	hold	Roll	
lab	lad	cag	ʃag	lips	ʃilk	cock	hops	Rome	
fab	mad	dag	rag	lint	ʃink	cold	horn	rote	
bad	nad	fag	tag	limn	ʃins	cork	host	roʃt	
dad	pad	hag	wag	list	ʃick	cord	John	rock	
	ʃad	jag	zag						

10.

Bob   cod
cob   GOD
fob
rob
gob
hob   Cold cock John for he holds the rock
job   of Rome's GOD.
mob
lob   Lick hops from ʃilk lips
            and link horns.

Oi and *Oy*, are generally hard; as in oil &c.

Let's speak of oil.
The import of brown children to learn
                                   the word
of GOD & OIL.

The indigen as obstacle. You will be removed.

Oil springs used by the autochthon
for medicinal purposes only.
Lubricated, we bring you up.
At what cost?

25,000 civilian casualties today, September 2005. The Oi in
oil
is generally hard.

Alaska. Iraq. You will be removed.

10.

Oil	coin	joint	toil	groin	coy
boil	loin	point	ſpoil	void	ſoy
coil	join	ſoil	broil	Boy	joy

       A coin slipped into an American Boy's joint
       to pay his toil, the ſpoils of which, are Oil.

Teach us the words we need
for our limited rhetoric—
Popiſh plots and Quranic crimes.

Oil for the machine.

Spiritual Milk
For American BABES.

Brant, did those little books drag us
from Wheelock's *worse than Egyptian darkness*?

At first, your libraries
from across the sea.

Little books taking root
and raining down when ripe:

An Account of a Plan for Civilising the North American
INDIANS.
A PRIMER For The USE of The MOHAWK CHILDREN.

The Original RIGHTS of MANKIND, Freely to Subdue
and Improve the EARTH.

The Duty of Christians toward the Heathen.

The Knowledge and Practice of CHRISTIANITY Made Easy to
the Meanest Capacities: Or an Easy Essay towards an Instruction
for the INDIANS.

Words too few
and biased for dialogue.

Brant, you knew:

In the government you call civilised, the happiness of the people is constantly sacrificed to the splendour of empire; hence your code of civil and criminal laws have had their origins.

As Locke knew before you:

If we could speak of Things as they are, we must allow, that all the Art of Rhetorick, besides Order and Clearness, all the artificial and figurative applications of Words Eloquence hath invented, are for nothing else but to insinuate wrong Ideas, move the Passions, and therby mislead the Judgment; and so indeed are perfect cheat...

Ee has the Sound of *e* long; as in ***Bee, fee, eel,***
lee, see, flee, free,, knee, kneel, thee, three, teem, teeth,
beef, beer, been, feem, breed, creed, fteed, sweet, sweep,
leek, sleep, meek, seek, feel, heel, jeer, keel, keep, reel,
steel, deep, deer, peel, peep, peer, week, weep.

Seek Freedom from the teeth of their deep Creed.
Keep meek. Sleep with your heels in Sweet beer.

1953, scattered brochures over Indian lands
urge urban Indian living to
fill the drained grey cities.
Suburbs teem with green grass / blue pools.

Some brown body needs to fill the vacant housing.
Some white and winning body needs mineral rich lands.

Promise. FREEDOM from the tyranny of poverty,
Education.

Oo has the sound of *u* long in theſe words,
          coom, hood, moor, root, broom, ſchool.

          Come for the ſchools. Set Roots in the Hood.

Except in ***blood, flood***; which ſound like *u* short,
          As blud, flud. See the Exerciſe on Spelling.

          Yes, expect a Flowing of Blood.

Little books spread

Aerial propa/ganda
            /gation.

Little leaflets on the wind.

We wish only to liberate the people of Iraq from tyranny.
For your safety, return to your homes and live in peace.

Today, five American men with
a company called, *Custer Battles*
report
civilian abuse by contractors.

Corporate claims made on a country.

The lists.

Of Supplies:

Schenectady, 9th July 1766—

"2 oz Brass Wire
"I Dozn. Pipes
"1 White Shirt to Huron Chief
"1 B: Rum Tody to Do.
"6 Bowld Tody
"5 Pints Wine
"1 Qt. Spirits
"Cash for a Cow
"Do. Pd. the Butcher for Killing her
"3 oz thread
"25 Needles
"1 pint Maderia Wine to Pondiack
"10 bowls tody
"3 pair scizars
"½ Gall:rum

Rum to aid in the Celebration of their Infernal Pawaws.

Of Suppliers/Bid Contractors:

"1. Honeywell (R, K)
"2. Spectra Physics (K)
"3. Semetex (R)
"4. TI Coating (A, K)
"5. Unisys (A, K)
"6. Sperry Corp. (R, K)
"7. Tektronix (R, A)
"8. Rockwell (K)
"9. Leybold Vacuum Systems (A)
"10. Finnigan-MAT-US (A)
"11. Hewlett-Packard (A, R, K)
"12. Dupont (A)
"13. Eastman Kodak (R)
"14. American Type Culture Collection (B)
"15. Alcolac International (C)
"16. Consarc (A)
"17. Carl Zeiss—US (K)
"18. Cerberus (LTD) (A)
"19. Electronic Associates (R)
"20. International Computer Systems (A, R, K)

Legend:

A = nuclear program
B = bioweapons program
C = chemical weapons program
R = rocket program
K = conventional weapons, military logistics,
supplies at the Iraqi Defense Ministry and the
building of military plants.

Lucky (ARK)s beached on the slopes of Ararat.

Oh beautiful for corporate skies.
The ships landed. Laborers labored.

500 years later, the laborer devalued.
Individuals
becoming corporate.

Oprah out of order.

H A R P O (Entertainment Group)

Read about Oprah in Africa.

*Read about Matthew McConaughey's daily encounters with
Hurricane Katrina victims at Oprah.com.*

And Oprah gave every male child a soccer ball.

And Oprah gave every female child a black doll.

And Oprah was touched by Africa, till a design emergency
occurred in the tiling of her Chicago kitchen. Oprah regrets
she has to leave Africa.

We do what we can.
Or do we?

The Alphabet's out of Order.

It will never be the same.

He that ne'er learns our A, B, C,
For ever will a Blockhead be;
But he that learns theſe Letters fair
Shall have a Coach to take the Air.

B   Heaven to find,
       the BIBLE mind.

R   A Brown man from our Tanks did RUN,
       Never more to See the Sun.

C   A traffic Jam in Baghdad, they did Bar,
       by firing into a Civilian CAR.

D   The DELUGE drowned,
       the Earth around.

G   An Indian shot for holding a GLOVE,
       Mistook for a White child's hand they Loved.

X   Old XERXES did die,
       and ſo muſt I.

T   We are Full of Glory all,
       when we Want to TAKE, ethics Fall.

L   LOT fled to *Zoar*, Saw fiery *Shower*,
       on Sodom pour.

Z   ZACCHEUS he, did Climb the tree,
Our Lord to See.

N   Geo. Washington ordered the Six NATIONS dead,
and They were Burned asleep in Their Beds.

V   To Compensate for American lives,
Hiroshima was VAPORIZED.

Y   While YOUTH do Cheere,
Death may be Near.

J   JOB feels the Rod,
Yet bleſſes GOD.

M   In the Congo, MASSES of people Killed,
Our newspapers Already fill'd.

W   If they are WHITE,
all is Right.

H   My Book and HEART
Muſt never Part.

K   When KING Phillip, dead did lay,
the Puritans did Make their Way.

E   Queen ESTHER ſues
And ſaves the *Jews*.

F   Humiliation at Abu Ghraib,
Hath FAMOUS little Lindey made.

A   In ADAM's fall,
     We ſinned All.

U   Fighting for Oil UNDER Other's Sands,
     makes you Hated in Foreign Lands.

S   If you Teach them only SELF to See,
     They will Comprehend Liberty.

O   OPRAH heard the Poor's Pleas,
     and Gave them All new SUV's.

Q   QUEEN Elizabeth Found most fair,
     The Policies of young Tony Blaire.

P   The fiendish POPE, London Town
     in 1666 did Burn to the Ground.

Brant, I arrive in London
two hundred twenty-nine years
and two hundred fifty-eight
                              days later.

The city still here.
Gone, The Swan with Two Necks,
from where it was noted:

> To thoſe who study Human Nature, he affords very
> convincing proof of the tameneſs which education
> can produce upon the wildeſt Race.

No note made of me,
but those of close complexion. Today
fours bombs fail on three Tube trains
and the No. 26 bus.

Warren Street.   Shepard's Bush.   Oval.   Hackney.

A city, knee-jerk jumpy since 7 July.

(*Ea, Eo, Ie, Oa, Oe, Ui, Ue,*) are commonly called
improper Diphthongs; becauſe only one of the
Vowels is heard in the pronunciation, as in theſe
words following, where the Vowel *a* is lost.

Bread	deaf	eaſe	cream
breath	Eal	each	cheap
dead	Eat	earth	bleat, Etc.

> The eaſe on this earth, with which
> deaf Ears breed cheap Death.

One day later,
a twenty-seven year old
Brazilian electrician shot Dead outside
the Stockwell Tube,
for turning a deaf Ear to police.

Not taking the time
to study the fold above his eyes,
a bystander says of the mistake:

*We are sorry and sincerely hope this will not make Asian
men afraid to come to London.*

It is 3 hours before the BBC reports, the man shot seven
times in the head and once in the shoulder was Brazilian.

Jean Charles de Menezes.

17.
Knee-jerk
Genuflect
Itchy-finger
trigger-Happy

An Essay towards an Instruction
for the Indians.

Miſſ. 'Who was CAIN?'
Ind. 'ADAM'S firft born Son, and he
killed his Brother Abel.'

Miſſ. 'What was ABEL?'
Ind. ' A better Man than Cain and there-
fore Cain hated him.

And still these words,
these alphabets of letters

fill   the   air

      on   waves,   internet,   ethernet.

Only the words we need to know,
spoonfed milk for American Babes.

Terror.   Security.   Orange alert.   Borders.

Fox news airs a weeklong special on
what is found
on shopping cart handles.

What Do You Pick Up at the Supermarket?

staphylococcus   influenza
cocaine   hemoflagellate
streptococcus   saliva
semen   hepatitis

The reasons, in general, I don't lick people when I meet
them or objects I encounter in any room.
Still there is affection
and it's brave language…

Brant had selected a bosom friend, in the person of a Lieutenant Provost…Those unacquainted with Indian usages are not probably aware of the intimacy, or the importance attached to this relationship. The selected friend is, in fact, the counterpart of the one who chooses him, and the attachment often becomes romantic; they share each other's secrets, and are participants of each other's joys and sorrows.

Provost ordered
off to the tropical West Indies.
Brant, in lament, sends a suit of finest fur.

Do not be so sorrowful, said Dr. Stewart, **Console
yourself with another friend—myself, for instance.**

No, said Brant, **I cannot do that. I am Captain John's
friend, and a transfer of my affections
cannot take place.**

And yet there is the body,
the bravest book.

13.

Words of Two Syllables.
    Tekaweanake.

Words of three Syllables.
    Aghfea Nikaweanake.

ohna'	skin	otskwe:na'	chest
o:stien	bones	oka:ra'	eyes
ohsa'	lips	onon'kwis	hair
		Awe:ri	Heart
		okwitsha'	knee
		onion'sa	nose
		onia:ra'	neck
		oho:kwa	buttoks
		ohnitsha'	thigh
		En'nahson	Tongue

Words of Four Syllables.
  Kayeri Nikaweanake.

oronhkwe:na'	back
onase:ta'	muscles
Onekwen:ta	Stomach
ohnhoskwa:rha'	hip

Ten days before leaving for London,
I choose my bosom friend,
now gone to Hyères.

Today, I'll weave a hair shirt
from our sheets
and send it to the south of France.

You call and
leave a message on my machine,
greet me in Mohawk.
Seh:kon.

I call back and you're not there.
I want to list the words for
the parts of your body.

You write and tell me, *Coucou*, is the word for hello.
You call and say, *Bisous*, is the word for kiss.

And these words
make bearable all others,

the warrings and warnings.

Trusting more the text of touch,
even bed bespoke words

can be perfect cheat.

The rivers of alphabets
beneath your skin.

The **A** of an Adam's Apple against the lips.
The **B** at the small of your Back, tapering at the hip.
The **C** of the Clavicle, a hollow for the thumb.

Too entangled in the naming of objects
and the namer, to trust the word
                        or the object.

By any and every day's end,
I know not whether a wineglass
                    is as strong as an iron.

Or whether any body
                speaks as true as an angle.

Brant, lettered Chief,
you saw it in its infancy.
Opened the book
                and understood.

An Alphabet out of Order.

B R C D G X T L Z N V Y I J M W H K E F A
U S O Q P

It would never be the same.

CPSIA information can be obtained
at www.ICGtesting.com
Printed in the USA
LVHW111722230921
698576LV00007B/1266